REALLY WILD REPTILES

CHAMELEONS

by Kathleen Connors

Please visit our website, www.garethstevens.com. For a free color catalog of all our high-quality books, call toll free 1-800-542-2595 or fax 1-877-542-2596.

Library of Congress Cataloging-in-Publication Data

Connors, Kathleen.
 Chameleons / Kathleen Connors.
     p. cm. — (Really wild reptiles)
 Includes index.
 ISBN 978-1-4339-8360-3 (pbk.)
 ISBN 978-1-4339-8361-0 (6-pack)
 ISBN 978-1-4339-8359-7 (library binding)
 1. Chameleons—Juvenile literature. I. Title.
 QL666.L23C66 2013
 597.95'6—dc23
                                                    2012018916

First Edition

Published in 2013 by
Gareth Stevens Publishing
111 East 14th Street, Suite 349
New York, NY 10003

Designer: Ben Gardner
Editor: Kristen Rajczak

Photo credits: Cover, p. 1 Iarus/Shutterstock.com, pp. 5, 9, 13 Cathy Keifer/Shutterstock.com; p. 7 Alan Lagadu/Shutterstock.com; p. 11 almondd/Shutterstock.com; p. 15 mikeledray/Shutterstock.com; p. 17 Peter Wey/Shutterstock.com; p. 19 Suzanne L and Joseph T. Collins/Photo Researchers/Getty Images; p. 20 Lipowski Milan/Shutterstock.com; p. 21 © iStockphoto.com/Studio-Annika.

Printed in the United States of America

CPSIA compliance information: Batch #CW13GS: For further information contact Gareth Stevens, New York, New York at 1-800-542-2595.

Contents

Words in the glossary appear in **bold** type the first time they are used in the text.

MEET THE CHAMELEON

Even among cool **reptiles** like crocodiles and boa constrictors, chameleons stand out. That's because these amazing lizards can change color!

There are more than 100 species, or kinds, of chameleons living around the world—and scientists are still finding more. Chameleons can be tiny, such as the *Brookesia micra*, which is only about an inch (2.5 cm) long. Parson's chameleon can grow to about 27 inches (69 cm) long! While some chameleons look flashier than others, they're all wild in other ways!

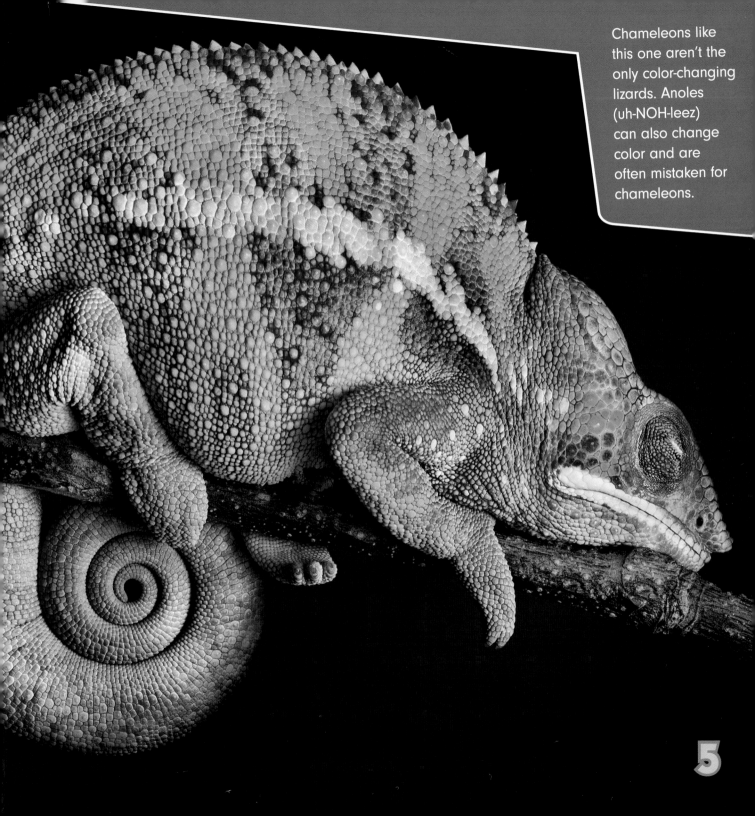

Chameleons like this one aren't the only color-changing lizards. Anoles (uh-NOH-leez) can also change color and are often mistaken for chameleons.

FANCY FEET

Like many other reptiles, chameleons have scales. The scales are commonly green, brown, or gray when the chameleon is at rest. Chameleons have two big eyes, and most have a long tail. They have zygodactylous (zy-guh-DAK-tuh-luhs) feet, which means two of their toes are stuck together facing forward and the other three are stuck together facing backward. No other lizard has feet like these!

Another cool feature of the chameleon is its long tongue. It can be almost twice the length of the animal's body!

Chameleons use their zygodactylous feet to climb trees.

What a Wild Life!

Chameleons can move each of their eyes independently as well as together. Their eyes are able to turn and look almost all the way behind the chameleon's head.

7

QUICK-CHANGE ARTISTS

The chameleon's famous color change happens in **cells** under their skin. These cells have **pigment** in them. The chameleon's body increases and decreases the size of certain pigment cells to change color.

Chameleons change color in response to how hot or cold it is, the time of day, and their mood. For example, if a chameleon is cold, it will increase the size of dark-colored pigment cells to turn black. The darker color takes in more heat than lighter colors to make the chameleon warmer!

What a Wild Life!

A chameleon's pigment cells are called chromatophores (kroh-MAT-uh-fors). Chromatophores may have yellow, blue, or white pigment in them.

Chameleons often change color when they feel scared, angry, or when meeting a **mate**. They can change to yellow, brown, or blue, or even become spotted!

Chameleons can be found in Africa, Spain, India, and Sri Lanka. The island of Madagascar, located off the southeast coast of Africa, has the largest chameleon population in the world. In fact, about half of chameleon species live only in Madagascar.

Forests are the most common chameleon **habitat**. Chameleons spend a lot of their time in trees and bushes. Unfortunately, people are clearing many chameleon habitats. Most kinds of these lizards aren't in trouble, but if we don't keep their habitats safe, chameleons could become **endangered**.

This Namaqua chameleon hunts for its food in the sand and rocks of the desert.

What a Wild Life!

Unlike other chameleon species, the Namaqua (nuh-MAH-kwuh) chameleon lives in one of the hottest and driest places in the world—the Namib Desert in Africa.

FOOD GRAB

Chameleons eat mostly bugs. They sit in a tree or bush and wait until their sharp eyes see a cricket or grasshopper coming by. Then, their long tongue flies out to catch it.

The end of a chameleon's tongue, which is tacky and looks like a suction cup, sticks to the bug and brings it back into the lizard's waiting mouth. Do you want to see a chameleon catch its dinner? Don't blink! Their tongues move faster than we can see.

What a Wild Life!
Big chameleons can catch young birds with their superfast, strong tongue.

This panther chameleon is using its amazing tongue to catch a cricket.

HIDING FROM HUNTERS

While chameleons' color-changing ability isn't used for **camouflage**, many chameleons' resting color blends in with the greens and browns of tree life. Their bodies are also somewhat flat on the sides, and small chameleons may look like leaves!

However, that doesn't always keep chameleons safe. Birds and snakes, especially those that hunt at night, are common chameleon **predators**. Some chameleon species have spines, or sharp points, down their back that could hurt an animal trying to have a chameleon meal.

What a Wild Life!

Many predators eat baby chameleons soon after they've **hatched**.

The Jackson's chameleon has three scary-looking horns it may use to try to keep predators away.

15

LEAVE ME ALONE!

Chameleons like to live alone. They only come together to mate, which can happen up to three times a year. Males change to bright colors like purple or blue to ask a female if she wants to mate.

Female chameleons change color to show they don't want to mate! They might hiss at a male that comes close, too. However, when a female chameleon is ready to mate, she won't change color. This lets the male know he can approach her.

What a Wild Life!

The male chameleons of some species have a red dewlap, or flap of skin under their throat. They show this to females when they want to mate.

Colorful chameleons may be trying to find a mate.

A few species of chameleons grow in eggs that hatch inside their mother's body! However, most chameleons hatch from eggs their mother has buried. The number of eggs in each clutch, or group of eggs, depends on the species of the chameleon. Some females lay as many as 100 eggs!

Baby chameleons grow in their eggs for 4 to 12 months. Mother chameleons leave their offspring to hatch on their own. After hatching, baby chameleons start to look for bugs to eat.

What a Wild Life!

One kind of chameleon, the Malagasy chameleon, spends 8 to 9 months in its egg, but only lives 4 to 5 months after hatching.

CHAMELEON PETS

Do you think chameleons are cool? You can keep this wild reptile as a pet! However, chameleon pets are often born in **captivity**.

These lizards need a lot of care. Have a big tank for your chameleon, as it will need lots of space to grow. The tank must not be kept too hot or too cold, and you'll need to give the chameleon bugs to eat. During a period of growth, your pet might eat 15 or 20 crickets in a day!

What a Wild Life!

By feeding them their favorite foods from a young age, chameleons can get used to you. However, some chameleons will never want you to touch them.

Cool Chameleon Features

spines to harm predators

color-changing skin to keep cool and show mood

long tongue to catch bugs

zygodactylous feet to climb trees

GLOSSARY

camouflage: colors or shapes that allow an animal to hide in its surroundings

captivity: the state of being caged

cell: the smallest, basic part of a living thing

endangered: in danger of dying out

habitat: the natural place where an animal or plant lives

hatch: to break open or come out of

mate: one of two animals that come together to make babies. Also, to come together to make babies.

pigment: the matter that gives something color

predator: an animal that hunts other animals for food

reptile: an animal covered with scales or plates that breathes air, has a backbone, and lays eggs, such as a turtle, snake, lizard, or crocodile

FOR MORE INFORMATION

Books

Petrie, Kristin. *Chameleons.* Minneapolis, MN: ABDO Publishing Company, 2013.

Thomas, Isabel. *Remarkable Reptiles.* Chicago, IL: Raintree Publishing, 2013.

Websites

Reptiles: Baby Chameleons

video.nationalgeographic.com/video/kids/animals-pets-kids/reptiles-kids/chameleon-babies-kids/

Watch baby chameleons hatch from their eggs and search for food.

Reptiles: Chameleon

www.sandiegozoo.org/animalbytes/t-chameleon.html
Read more about chameleons and see many pictures of this amazing lizard.

INDEX